BUT WHY

ARE LLAMAS TICKLISH?

AND OTHER SILLY QUESTIONS FROM CURIOUS KIDS

BUT WHY

ARE LLAMAS TICKLISH?

AND OTHER SILLY QUESTIONS FROM CURIOUS KIDS

by Jane Lindholm and Melody Bodette
illustrations by Neil Swaab

GROSSET & DUNLAP

GROSSET & DUNLAP
An imprint of Penguin Random House LLC, New York

First published in the United States of America by Grosset & Dunlap,
an imprint of Penguin Random House LLC, New York, 2022

Text copyright © 2022 by Jane Lindholm and Melody Bodette

Illustrations on the following pages copyright © 2022 by Neil Swaab: cover, iii, iv, viii–1,
3 (cow), 4, 7, 12, 16, 17, 20, 21, 27, 31, 32–33, 35 (pepper, seeds), 36, 37, 45 (corn), 47,
48 (human, sheep), 49 (chicken, goat), 57, 61, 64–65, 66–67 (flies), 70, 76, 85 (clouds),
86–87, 94, 102, 103, 104–105, 113 (moose), 114, 116–117, 124–125, 130

Author photo on page vii by Jane Lindholm and Melody Bodette

Photos and illustrations not listed above are from Getty Images.

GROSSET & DUNLAP is a registered trademark of Penguin Random House LLC.

Visit us online at penguinrandomhouse.com.

Library of Congress Cataloging-in-Publication Data is available.

Manufactured in China

ISBN 9780593384343   10 9 8 7 6 5 4 3 2 1 TOPL

CONTENTS

INTRODUCTION

DO YOU KNOW WHY GOATS HAVE RECTANGULAR EYES?
Why horses sleep standing up? Or if llamas laugh when they're tickled? Welcome to the first-ever *But Why* book! We'll help you get to know some interesting facts about farm animals by answering questions real kids have sent us.

But Why started out as a podcast for curious kids, produced by Vermont Public Radio and made by us, Melody Bodette and Jane Lindholm. We take questions from kids all over the world and it's our job to find answers. And now *But Why* is a book series, too!

Maybe we should start by defining what it means to call something a farm animal. Generally speaking, farm animals have been domesticated, meaning they've been bred and adapted over time to be cared for and used by humans. Domesticated animals are no longer considered wild, and, in many cases, couldn't survive on their own. Animals have lots of different jobs on a farm. Some pull machinery or

? BUT WHY

heavy loads (these are called draft animals), and some, like horses, are used as transportation to help people get around. Their hair or fur can be used to make clothes and other materials, their composted poop can help grow vegetables, their eggs or milk can be used for food, and sometimes the animals themselves become food for humans.

There are lots of different kinds of farm animals, and we won't have time in this book to get to all of them. But we hope you'll have a greater understanding of the importance of farm animals and their roles in how you get your food by the time you finish this book!

And if you still have questions when you're done reading, send them our way and we'll see if we can include them in a future podcast episode or book!

Go to page 136 to learn more about how to send in your own questions. In the meantime, stay curious!

CHAPTER 1

COWS AND THE CURIOUS WAY MILK IS MADE

?

WHY DO COWS MAKE MILK?

—COCO, 7, ILLINOIS

GREAT QUESTION, COCO! THE SHORT ANSWER IS THIS:
Cows make milk because they are mammals. But what exactly is a mammal? A mammal is an animal who feeds from the breast of its mother. The word *mammal* comes from *mamma*, the Latin word for breast.

What makes mammals different from other types of animals? Well, to begin with, they are warm-blooded vertebrates. This means they keep their bodies at a consistent temperature, no matter how warm or cold it is outside. Also, they have spines. Mammals have hair or fur and give birth to live babies—instead of laying eggs, for example. And as we mentioned, females produce milk in special mammary glands to feed those babies.

HELLO!

That means humans are mammals, too! And so are nearly 6,500 other kinds of animals, including cats, dogs, elephants, kangaroos, dolphins, and even whales.

In humans, the mammary glands are in what we call breasts. In cows, we call them udders, or sometimes bags—because if you've ever seen a cow's udder, it kind of looks like a heavy bag hanging down between the cow's back legs! Cows' udders have four teats, which are like long nipples. Baby cows, called calves, will drink their milk from those nipples.

But as you likely know, it's not just calves that drink cow's milk—humans do, too! Dairy cows usually give birth to a calf once a year. Shortly after they're born, most calves are separated from their mothers and fed formula from a big bottle that gives them all the nutrients they need to grow.

The milk from the mother cow becomes the milk, yogurt, butter, and cheese that you buy in the store.

After a cow has given birth, she's usually milked twice a day for the rest of the year. Then, she gets ready to have another calf, and the process begins again. Some farms may actually milk their cows three times a day, and some very small farms may only milk their cows once a day. Dairy cows can produce as much as seven or eight gallons of milk a day! It takes a lot of energy to produce all that milk. Cows drink as much as a bathtub full of water every day! And they eat lots of hay, grass, and grains.

Families with just one or two cows might milk their cows by hand. But dairy farms use machines to milk the cows. On some farms, the milking is actually done by robotic machines, and cows can even choose for themselves when to be milked! Most milking machines look kind of like a little octopus with four cups that go over the cow's teats. The machine squeezes and pulls the teats in a rhythmic way, drawing the milk out of the cow's teats similar to the way a baby calf might suck the milk out. But don't worry! Milking doesn't hurt the cows.

The milk flows through a system of tubes and pipes into a big container, called a bulk tank, where milk from all the different cows gets mixed together and cooled down.

But there are still a few more steps before the milk gets to you. Most milk is pasteurized (say: PAST-your-ized), which means it gets heated up really quickly to kill any bacteria, and then cooled back down before the milk can cook.

Milk also goes through something called homogenization (say: huh-MAH-je-ne-ZAY-shun). Raw milk naturally separates—the thick fatty cream rises to the top and the thinner milk sinks to the bottom—kind of like how oil and water poured into a glass separate into two distinct layers. Homogenization is the process in which fat molecules are broken down so that milk and cream can combine. This is why you don't have to shake or stir it back together before

drinking. But if you've ever had "skim milk," it's called that because the cream has been "skimmed" from the top, leaving only the less fatty milk behind.

WHY DO WE DRINK COW'S MILK, INSTEAD OF OTHER MAMMALS' MILK?—ADRIA, 5, CONNECTICUT

WHILE HUMAN BABIES HAVE ALWAYS DRUNK THEIR OWN mother's milk, we developed a taste for the milk of other animals less than ten thousand years ago—which is pretty recent in the span of human history! For most of human evolution, adults couldn't drink milk at all—it would make them a little sick. But at some point, people discovered they could eat foods like cheese and butter, which are made from milk, without getting sick. So, they started milking cows, buffalo, camels, and other mammals they had domesticated. And right around that time, some humans developed a mutation that allowed them to keep drinking milk into adulthood! It's all about lactase (say: LACK-tays), a special enzyme (say: en-ZIME; a natural substance that creates a chemical reaction in your body) that breaks down the sugar in milk.

And humans don't just drink cow's milk. Sheep's milk and goat's milk are also popular, especially when made into yogurt or cheese. People around the world drink yak, horse, reindeer, llama, and camel milk!

WHY IS MILK WHITE?

—VEDANT, 6, CALIFORNIA

GREAT QUESTION, VEDANT! WHAT COLOR WOULD YOU PREFER?

Purple milk would be cool!

To begin with, the color of milk has a lot to do with physics and a little to do with chemistry. Physics is the scientific study of matter, motion, and energy. Chemistry is how matter (stuff) reacts with other matter (other stuff).

To get the details, we visited the Billings Farm & Museum in Woodstock, Vermont, where we met Christine Scales, who runs educational programs for the working farm. She showed us the herd of about seventy Jersey cows they keep at the farm.

Billings Farm is just like the farm you might see in a children's book: rolling green pastures and lots of animals! In addition to cows, they have draft horses, pigs, goats, sheep, and chickens. Their mission is to teach people about farming and history. It's a great place for people to learn, and if you've never seen a cow in person, a Jersey is a great first cow to meet. Jerseys are a beautiful soft gray-brown color, and they're known to be very friendly cows!

Their milk is known for having more fat in it than other types of cows' milk. A higher fat content means their milk is rich and creamy, and often used for butter, cheese, and ice cream. Milk fat plays an important role in why milk is white!

Here's where the chemistry comes into play:

"Milk looks white to us because of the fat in the milk and also because of the protein called casein that's in the milk," Christine Scales explained. Milk is about 87 percent water, but it also contains a sugar called lactose and minerals like calcium. There are also several kinds of proteins in milk, but the main one is called casein (say: KAY-seen). The casein and calcium join together to form little clusters called micelles (say: my-SELLS). When light shines through milk, it hits the micelles and all the light gets scattered, which is what makes the milk look white.

Whoa! Okay, that's a lot of information to take in. But wait . . . there's even more! Here's how physics plays a role in the color of milk:

When light hits an object, some of it is absorbed by the object and some reflects back to us. The light that bounces back tells us what color the object is. And when *all* of the light is reflected back at us, that object appears white.

The micelles in milk—the protein and mineral clusters—reflect almost all light, making the milk appear white.

(If your head is spinning now, that's totally understandable.)

Not all milk is exactly the same color! "If you've ever seen skim milk next to maybe a whole fat milk," Scales points out, "it might actually look a little bit more bluish because it doesn't have the fats in it to make it look white." So milk with less fat in it can look blue. And heavy cream, with a *lot* of fat in it, can actually look kind of yellow!

DO BROWN COWS MAKE CHOCOLATE MILK?

Sadly, no! Chocolate milk does not come from brown cows, despite what some people might think. All cows produce white milk. So even though the Jerseys at Billings Farm & Museum have a nice chocolaty color on the outside, their milk is just as white as any other cow's. The flavorings that make milk taste chocolaty are added after the milk comes out of the cow. No strawberry milk from pink cows, either, though it's fun to imagine!

If milk comes from mammals, what's the deal with soy, almond, rice, or even oat milk? Those aren't mammals—they're not even animals! Drinks from these plants are made by soaking soybeans, almonds, rice, or oats in water and then grinding the mixture up and squeezing out the liquid to make a drink. These drinks are made as plant-based alternatives to milk. Some people drink these because they can't drink cow's milk, and some people would rather not eat or drink animal products like cow's milk.

Some people think these alternative milks are healthier, but that's not necessarily true. Some contain a lot of sugar and might not have the same amount of protein and nutrients as cow's milk.

And when it comes to whether or not plant-based milk is better for the environment, again that depends on which kind of plant milk you choose! Some crops require more land and water than dairy milk, others require less. If you're considering switching to plant milk, it's important to do your homework!

WHY DO SOME ANIMALS EAT GRASS?—COLTON, 5, CALIFORNIA

JUST LIKE YOU, COLTON, ALL ANIMALS NEED TO EAT!

But not all animals eat the same food . . .

Animals that mostly eat meat, or other animals, are called carnivores. Animals that primarily eat plants are called herbivores. Animals that eat both meat and plants are called omnivores. Humans are omnivores (though some people choose to just eat plants).

And here's a vocabulary word you might not know! Animals that eat mostly grass are called graminivores! This word comes from two Latin words: *graminis*, meaning "grass," and *vorare*, meaning "to eat." When animals eat grass, we call this grazing. Cows, sheep, and some other hoofed animals are graminivores. And some birds and insects are, too!

Joel McNair is the editor of *Graze*, a magazine all about the farm animals

TASTY!

that eat grass. "Farm animals like cows and sheep have four stomachs that are specifically designed to digest grasses and other plants that can't be eaten by humans," McNair says. "These four-stomached animals can grow and be very happy eating things that would make people sick." That's right! Some graminivores have *four* stomachs!

CHOMP
CHOMP
CHOMP

These animals, called ruminants (say: ROOM-uh-nintz), include cows, goats, sheep, deer, buffalo, and antelope. When they rip the grass from the ground (or pick up hay or other grass that they're fed on the farm), they don't spend a lot of time chewing it into small pieces. Instead, they give the grass a few quick chews and then swallow it down into their first stomach.

There, chemicals called enzymes help break the grass into smaller, pulpy pieces. Once that grass has broken down a little bit, the animal actually regurgitates it. Regurgitation is kind of like throwing up in your mouth. Gross, right? Well, to us, yes, but for these animals it's all part of the process!

The animal takes that ball of wet, pulpy grass, called cud, and chews it again! Once the grass is chewed up into smaller, wetter pieces, it's easier to digest and it can go through the rest of the animal's digestive system, where all the nutrients get into the bloodstream and give the animal the energy it needs to roam and play.

This might seem like quite a lot of work to go through just to eat some grass. Some farms feed grain to their graminivores in addition to grass and hay, but Joel McNair says eating grass is what their bodies are specially designed to do. "Grass is healthier for cows. They don't get upset stomachs eating grass like they do when they eat too much grain. Their digestive systems are designed for grass, not grain."

MOOOOO
MOOOOO

Letting farm animals roam around and graze takes a lot of land. But many experts say it's actually better for the environment than growing grains like corn and soybeans.

"Grazing and grass keep the soil in place so it doesn't wash away into the rivers and lakes and make them dirty," Joel McNair says. "Grass doesn't need chemicals to grow, so fewer chemicals soak into the water that people drink."

Still, not all graminivores have four stomachs. Horses have only one stomach, like humans. However, unlike humans, they have those special enzymes in their stomachs to help break down the grass, so that their bodies can use it for energy.

And even though humans don't actually eat grass, much of the food we eat depends on it!

THE GRASS-EATING GRASSHOPPER

Lots of farm animals eat grass. And wild animals who you might see grazing in fields, like deer, elk, and buffalo, are graminivores. So are giraffes, capybara, hippos, and kangaroos. Some fish are graminivores, and so are most geese. But even some insects munch on grass, like grasshoppers! Grasshoppers are normally pretty harmless, solitary creatures that don't do much damage. But some grasshoppers, under the right conditions, have a change in the chemicals in their bodies that makes them breed rapidly and form huge groups called swarms. These grasshoppers are known as locusts, and when they gather together, they can cause tremendous damage to farm crops!

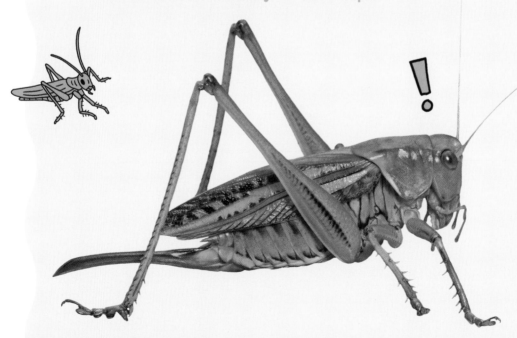

Grasshoppers themselves are also good sources of protein and are eaten by people all over the world. As many as eighty different species of grasshoppers are collected for food. And if you live in Oaxaca, Mexico, you might enjoy *chapulines*, roasted grasshoppers seasoned with lime, salt, and other flavors.

CHAPTER 2
PIGS AND THE PUZZLING TALE OF THE CURLY TAIL

WHY DO PIGS HAVE MORE TEATS THAN COWS?—KIERAN, 4, VIRGINIA

WELL, KIERAN, PIGS HAVE MORE TEATS—ANOTHER WORD for an animal's nipples—than cows because they tend to have more babies at a time than cows do.

Cows usually give birth to one calf, sometimes two, and have four teats. Pigs, on the other hand, can have litters of ten or more piglets and have many more teats than cows do, to be able to feed most or all of their piglets at the same time.

The number of teats can vary from pig to pig. Some have as few as eight nipples and others have had as many as twenty! This doesn't necessarily guarantee that pig will have twenty piglets, but more piglets are likely to survive in big litters if the mother pig, called a sow, has enough teats for all of them to nurse at once. Some farmers breed their pigs to have more teats on purpose.

AWWW

Interestingly, it's quite common to have variety in the number of teats or nipples—even in humans! While most goats have two teats, some have four and occasionally they have three. Cows sometimes have an extra, smaller teat that doesn't work. Pigs, as we've learned, have a lot of variation. And even humans can sometimes have more than two nipples, though usually only two of them are functional for milk production. And even though only the females produce milk, most male mammals still have nipples, or teats, but they're usually quite a bit smaller.

So, Kieran, if you see an animal with lots of teats, it probably means they tend to have lots of babies at the same time.

AW!

WHY DO PIGS HAVE CURLY TAILS?

—HOLDEN, 6, CALIFORNIA

THAT'S ACTUALLY A BIT OF A MYSTERY, HOLDEN!

Some scientists think that when people started domesticating pigs, some of them had curly tails and some didn't. Farmers try to select animals with certain traits, like lots of teats or more fat or certain colors. If you put two animals with that trait together to have offspring (babies), those offspring are also more likely to have that trait. This is called selective breeding. So, it's likely that people breeding pigs selected ones with curly tails. But researchers aren't sure whether the farmers did that on purpose, or if they were selecting pigs for other traits, and those pigs happened to have curly tails.

Christine Scales of Billings Farm & Museum in Woodstock, Vermont, says, "When pigs are born, they actually have straight tails! And then their tails curl as they get older." And not all pigs have curly tails! Most wild pigs and some domesticated pigs have straight tails.

Like dogs, pigs can wag their tails, and sometimes even curly-tailed pigs will straighten their tails out in stressful environments. Pig researchers are still trying to understand more about the relationship between pigs' tails and their moods.

PIGS: THE ORIGINAL RECYCLERS

Pigs are great recyclers, and will eat just about anything! People who keep a few backyard pigs often feed them kitchen scraps or waste milk or other things destined for the trash or compost. And since most pigs are raised to be eaten, this is an efficient way to turn food waste into more food!

Having a sustainable small-scale farming operation means all the different aspects of the farm work together. Pigs will eat the leftover food scraps and their poop can be used as fertilizer to grow vegetables, and eventually the pigs themselves become food.

YUM!

Pigs are also very useful to farmers because they can be used to clear land that can then become pasture for other animals. Pigs will use their snouts (noses) to root around in  the dirt to eat, well, roots! And also grubs (small insects that live in the dirt). Those snouts are kind of like a garden rototiller, a machine that turns over soil before crops are planted in it. Once the pigs have cleared an area, farmers can plant cover crops (grasses, rye, and clover) and use the land as a pasture for their other animals.

WHY DO PIGS LIKE MUD?
—ARCHER, 5, CALIFORNIA

YOU MIGHT HAVE BEEN TOLD, AT ONE POINT OR ANOTHER, that your room looks like a pigsty! A sty is another word for a pigpen—the fenced-in area where pigs live. Or maybe you've heard some other expression that suggests that pigs are dirty and messy. Many cartoons have poked fun at filthy pigs.

In fact, nothing could be further from the truth! Pigs are tidy animals. They usually pick one spot in their pigpen as a bathroom, and they like to keep things pretty neat.

They *do* like to roll in mud, but not because they like to be dirty.

OINK
OINK

It's to keep their skin cool and covered. The mud acts kind of like sunscreen to prevent sunburns. And rolling around in muddy water helps to keep them cool on hot days. Have you ever heard anyone say they are "sweating like a pig"? Well, next time someone says that, you can let that person know pigs can't sweat!

CHAPTER 3
A (BRIEF) HISTORY OF FARMING

HOW HAS AGRICULTURE CHANGED THE WORLD?

—JANE & MELODY, AGES UNKNOWN, VERMONT

OKAY, SO THIS QUESTION DIDN'T COME IN FROM A KID LIKE YOU, but we think it's an important one!

Have you ever wondered why people do the jobs that they do? For instance, why are some people farmers and others are not? And have you ever wondered how and when humans became reliant on animals for food, fur, and draft power? To answer these questions, we'll have to journey deep, *deep* into the past, to a time before civilization

For most of human history, we were what are known as hunter-gatherers. We spent our days in pursuit of food—foraging for nuts, fruit, and other wild plants. We also hunted wild animals. Most people were nomadic, meaning they moved around a lot instead of having a permanent

home or settlement. They likely had to move to follow the growing seasons and the changing habits of the animals on which they relied.

They noticed that they could control where plants grew by gathering seeds and planting them in the right kind of soil. This discovery meant that they could grow their own fruits and vegetables—farming—instead of relying on wild plants for food. They didn't need to go back to the same place each year to find fruits and vegetables; they could take seeds and plant crops wherever they wanted.

So, starting about twelve thousand years ago, groups of people started experimenting with growing crops and herding animals. And it was only around seven thousand years ago that people began staying in one place for their whole lives, to raise their own animals and grow fruits, vegetables, and grains as their main source of food. Once they no longer had to roam to find food, people started building homes and other solid structures, and creating permanent settlements.

Archaeologists (say: aar-KEE-ah-luh-juhst) and anthropologists, people who research human history and behavior, have a few ideas about why these groups of people decided to stay put. It's possible that over-hunting had made large animals harder to find. Or there may have been changes to the climate that affected people's ability to forage. Even if we don't know exactly why these people settled down, it's clear that the invention of agriculture changed human civilization.

WHO INVENTED FARMING?

WHO WERE THESE EARLY FARMERS? WELL, THERE WASN'T one person, or even one group of people, who could be called the first farmers. The change happened slowly, and it may have happened in several different places simultaneously (that means at the same time). Archaeologists think agricultural practices were developed in China, South America, and the Middle East, all around the same time.

This was *way* before these groups of people could call or visit one another, so it's unlikely that people from one part of the world introduced farming to people from another. Somehow, they all made the shift to farming in the same time period, so there may have been a common cause.

Early crops in the Middle East were legumes, figs, and grains like wheat and barley. In China, rice and millet were grown. In South America, crops included squash and maize (corn). Over time, farming cultures developed new technologies to improve what they could grow. They learned about irrigation systems to keep plants watered, and fertilization to improve the soil.

Agriculture allowed ancient cities to grow in Egypt, South America, and China. And as the amount of food a community could grow improved, not everyone in that village or community had to focus on finding or cultivating food. So, while some people farmed, some began doing other jobs. And then they could barter, or trade, their skills or goods for food. Eventually, this barter system led to the creation of money.

WHAT WAS THE FIRST FARM ANIMAL?

AS HUMANS WERE LEARNING TO GROW DIFFERENT CROPS, they were also learning to live side by side with animals. That's known as domestication—taming a wild animal! The first domestic animal was the dog, a descendant of the wolf.

Scientists used to think that early humans captured and tamed wolves. But another idea is that dogs actually domesticated themselves. Wolves may have realized that humans had a lot of food scraps lying around. If they made themselves useful to humans by protecting them, they could have access to some of that food.

Cute, friendly wolves were more likely to be welcomed by humans, which helps explain why modern dogs don't look exactly like their wild cousins.

Dogs aren't farm animals, though; and they may have been living with humans for forty thousand years, way longer than humans have farmed! The first animals that we would really think of as domestic farm animals were likely sheep and goats, followed closely by cattle (cows). These animals were herded, not kept inside barns and fences like they are today. By domesticating animals, humans had another food source, and animal products like hides (skin) and fur could be turned into clothing, bags, rope, and other useful items. Cattle, sheep, and goats can also eat plants, like grass, that humans can't eat. When animals eat those plants, and humans eat the animals, humans can take advantage of the calories from grass and other plants that they can't digest themselves.

Researchers say there are basically fifteen species of large animals that are considered domesticated: goats, sheep, pigs, horses, and cows are the most widespread throughout the world. Others include donkeys, camels, llamas, reindeer, water buffalo, yaks, and two other types of cattle: gayal and Bali cattle.

How humans were able to turn some wild animals into domesticated ones is a puzzle scientists are actively trying to understand better, even today. Why can't we domesticate hippos or cockroaches or skunks? Most researchers think that to be domesticated by humans, an animal has to be of a practical size (so no domesticated rhinoceroses), willing and able to eat a variety of foods (sorry, koalas), have the right temperament (there go the hippos!), and be able to reproduce in captivity (no pandas). Just because an animal lives in a zoo doesn't mean it's domesticated.

And the process takes longer than you'd think! One research project in Russia has been working on domesticating foxes for over sixty years. After many generations of foxes were bred in captivity, the foxes in this project are no longer afraid of humans the way wild foxes usually are. In fact, these foxes now act more like dogs, and get excited to greet people.

HELLO!

Interestingly, these domestic foxes have also changed physically over the generations, even though the researchers weren't trying to make them look different. They now have spotted coats and curled tails. Baby foxes growing up in this group have ears that stay floppy, like a puppy's, for a longer time than wild fox pups' do. These domestic foxes still aren't ready to be pets, but this project has shown how animals can change when people get involved!

HOW HAS FARMING CHANGED US?

IF DOMESTICATION CHANGES HOW ANIMALS LOOK AND ACT, has farming changed humans? Considering that *homo sapiens* (humans) have only been around for two hundred thousand years, the shift to agriculture is actually very recent!

There are still groups of people who live nomadic or hunter-gatherer lifestyles in the world today, mostly in South America, Asia, and Africa. Some of these groups have never had contact with other human societies.

But the discovery of farming has led to massive changes in how most humans live.

Farming is the reason we live in solid houses, we have towns and cities, we have all kinds of different jobs, and we use money to buy and sell things. It's the reason we have so many people on Earth.

Most of us rely on other people to grow the food we eat, which gives us time to go to school, play with our friends, and do all the other things

we can focus on because we're not spending all of our time and resources finding food.

Increased food production has allowed the human population to grow. There may have been about four million people on Earth twelve thousand years ago, but with the help of agriculture, the population has grown to more than seven billion people now!

So we're probably not going back to hunting and gathering anytime soon. Some scientists estimate that the world could only support around ten million hunter-gatherers. We simply can't find enough calories in the wild to support all seven billion of us. So, while there are a lot of questions about how to support people *and* the natural resources of the land, we need farming to feed the world.

TIMELINE

HOMO
SAPIENS
EVOLVE

**200,000
YEARS AGO**

SHEEP
DOMESTICATED

**13,000–11,000
YEARS AGO**

COWS
DOMESTICATED

**10,500
YEARS AGO**

MOOOOO

**40,000–15,000
YEARS AGO**

**12,000
YEARS AGO**

BEGINNINGS OF
AGRICULTURE

DOGS
DOMESTICATED

WOOF!

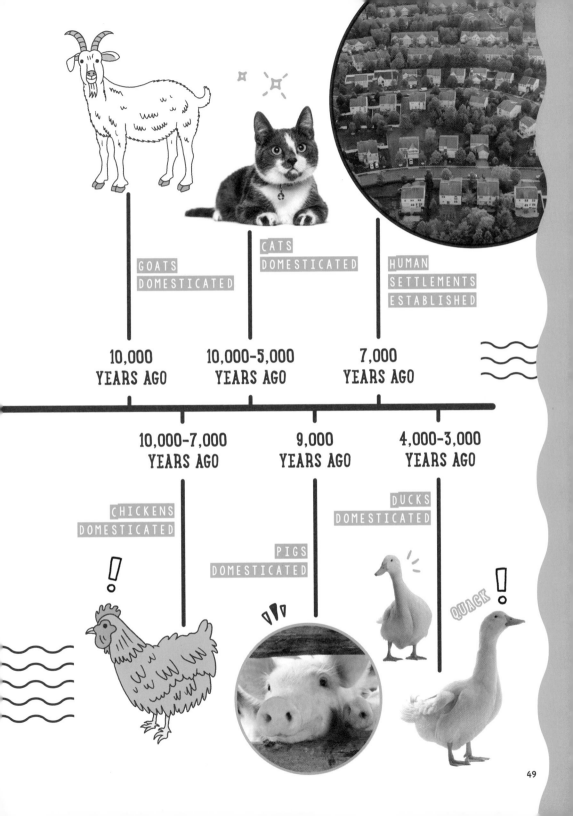

GOATS DOMESTICATED

CATS DOMESTICATED

HUMAN SETTLEMENTS ESTABLISHED

10,000
YEARS AGO

10,000–5,000
YEARS AGO

7,000
YEARS AGO

10,000–7,000
YEARS AGO

9,000
YEARS AGO

4,000–3,000
YEARS AGO

CHICKENS DOMESTICATED

PIGS DOMESTICATED

DUCKS DOMESTICATED

QUACK

CHAPTER 4
CHICKENS AND THE MYSTERIOUS PRODUCTION OF COLORFUL EGGS

?

WHY ARE SOME EGGS BROWN AND SOME WHITE? —MARINA, 8, FLORIDA

AS MARINA HAS NOTICED, DIFFERENT KINDS OF CHICKENS lay different colored eggs. Did you know that chicken breeds are as varied as dog breeds? Cat Parrish, who runs educational programs at a working farm and museum in Vermont called Shelburne Farms, says there are hundreds of breeds of chickens.

"Different chickens have different colored feathers, different patterns on their feathers. Some have extra toes. They have different colored skin. And just like all of these other differences, chickens lay different colored eggs as well," Parrish says. Most chicken eggs are some variety of white, brown, or blue-green.

But there's more to it than that. It takes a female chicken (called a hen) about twenty-six hours to lay an egg. First, the yolk forms. If the egg winds up fertilized, a baby chicken (a chick) will start to grow inside this yolk sac. The loose jelly-like egg white surrounds the yolk and provides nutrition to the developing bird. And the eggshell forms around the white to protect the delicate insides.

Most shells start out white. As the eggshell is forming, the egg is moving through the chicken. Before it leaves the chicken's body, it passes through a tube called the oviduct.

Inside the oviduct, there's something called a shell gland. Natural colors called pigments are in the shell gland. As the egg passes through, these natural pigments get layered onto the shell and turn it blue-green or reddish brown, or even a little bit speckled. Think of the chicken's body as an egg painting factory, where the longer an egg spends inside the body, the darker the egg will become.

"One chicken can also lay different shades of that

CLUCK **?**
CLUCK

same color," Parrish says. "So a chicken that lays dark brown eggs, depending on how fast the egg's traveling through her body and through the little pigment painting zone of her body, it could, if it travels through really fast, be a lighter color brown." Because the egg is moving fast, it has less time to get "painted." But when the chicken is laying at a slower pace, in the fall or winter, the eggs have more time in the oviduct and can turn out a little darker. How neat is that?

TWEET TWEET

As for why birds, including chickens, have such variety in the colors and patterns on their eggs, there are a lot of theories. For some birds, the specific color and pattern—any speckles or squiggles on the egg—might provide camouflage (say: KAH-mo-flazh), so predators have a harder time spotting an open nest. For birds that nest in rookeries (bird nurseries) with lots of other birds, those speckles, streaks, or squiggly lines might actually be used by the parents to identify their own eggs.

Another theory is that birds in colder climates are more likely to lay dark-colored eggs to help them stay warm, because darker colors absorb more heat than light ones. There's still a lot to be learned about the beautiful variety in eggs!

WHY AREN'T BLUE CHICKEN EGGS SOLD AT THE MARKET?

Mostly, markets don't sell blue eggs because that's not what people want to buy. Studies have shown that people in most parts of the United States prefer to buy white eggs, though people who live in New England prefer brown eggs.

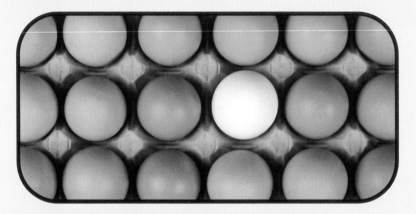

But there's another reason we don't see many blue eggs in stores: Egg farmers raise the types of chickens that produce the most eggs. The most common chicken that lays blue eggs is a breed called the Araucana. They lay around 150 eggs a year. Compare that with a chicken like the white leghorn, which can lay 250 to 300 eggs a year! Or a Rhode Island Red, which lays brown eggs, and lays about 250 eggs a year. There is a pretty new breed of chicken called the Ameraucana that lays up to 200 blue-green eggs per year, so maybe you'll start to see their eggs appear on your supermarket shelf someday. Would you like to buy blue-green eggs? Of course, blue-green eggs still look the same as other eggs on the inside. And the nutrition of eggs doesn't change based on shell color. Blue eggs aren't more or less healthy than brown or white eggs.

By the way, you probably keep your eggs in the refrigerator to keep them cold so that they don't spoil. But in other parts of the world, eggs might be kept on the counter. What gives?

In the United States, egg farmers have to wash their eggs with water before they can sell them in stores. This makes for clean eggs, but it also washes away a natural protective layer of the egg called the "bloom." Without this protective layer, the eggs must be refrigerated to be safe to eat.

In other countries, it's illegal for a farmer to wash eggs with water, making them safe to store on the counter for two weeks or so, bloom intact!

WHY DO CHICKENS LAY EGGS TO EAT, AND ALSO EGGS THAT BECOME CHICKS?—FRANCESCO, 7, OREGON

EGGS WILL ONLY TURN INTO CHICKS IF THEY'VE BEEN FERTILIZED (meaning genes from a rooster, a male chicken, were added to the egg before it was laid). So if you don't have a rooster, an egg can't turn into a chick. It takes just a few seconds for a hen and a rooster to mate, when they touch the parts of their bodies called a cloacae (say: clo-AY-kee) together.

If a hen lays an egg after mating with a rooster, her egg is likely to be fertilized and could hatch into a chick under the right conditions. That would require the hen to sit on the egg and keep it warm for the next twenty-one days. Or a human might put the egg into an incubator, a special container with a heat lamp that can keep the egg warm like a mother hen would.

If a fertilized egg is put into a refrigerator shortly after it's laid, the egg will be too cool for the chick inside to grow. You might just see a little red dot or some red webbing inside the yolk (the yellow part). It's perfectly safe to eat. However, older hens may also lay eggs with a red spot in the yolk because of their age, not because the eggs are fertilized. So don't worry if you see a red dot in your freshly cracked egg.

Many healthy hens lay an egg almost every day, especially in the warmer months, whether they're fertilized or not. But why would they lay eggs that have no chance of ever becoming chicks? That has to do with how long it takes to make an egg and when fertilization takes place in the process. An egg is almost ready to be laid before it has the chance to be fertilized, so the chicken has already done most of the work of producing it by that point, and the egg needs to come out one way or another!

Humans have figured out that those eggs are good to eat, and so most farmers keep hens to lay eggs, not to raise baby chickens. Over the years, farmers have tried to breed chickens that lay eggs more frequently. So that's why chickens lay so many eggs that never become chicks.

WHY DO ROOSTERS CROW?

—LAUREN, 8, MARYLAND

ROOSTERS CROW TO COMMUNICATE. MOST BIRDS SING, and for chickens, crowing is kind of like their way of singing, even though it might not sound like a very pretty song to us, Lauren!

Like many other birds, roosters sing first thing in the morning, when the light returns.

But contrary to popular belief, roosters don't just crow at sunrise. They'll crow if they're startled, or to sound an alarm, or to mark their territory. The sound of a rooster crowing is so familiar, even the littlest of kids learn to mimic the "cock-a-doodle-doo!"

But not everyone appreciates the loud and enthusiastic call. In some towns in the United States and elsewhere, it's actually illegal to have roosters, or to have more than one or two, because of how noisy they can be.

The joke might be on them, though, because hens can make just as much noise as roosters! If there's no rooster in a flock, sometimes a dominant hen develops a crow-like call, and will use it to sound an alarm. (Some towns ban all backyard chickens.)

Chicken flocks will establish a hierarchy, where certain hens have more power than others. That's also called a pecking order. The more dominant hens will literally peck other chickens in order to get to the food first or to get to the most desired roost or nesting box. This privilege comes with responsibility, though. The top chicken needs to be alert for predators and warn the rest of the flock.

If you do have a rooster that's a little too loud for the neighborhood, there are actually companies that advertise special collars to keep the rooster from being quite so loud! Some of these devices are made to look like little bow ties, so your backyard rooster can be fancy *and* quiet.

SNAZZY

CHAPTER 5
LLAMAS AND SHEEP AND GOATS . . . OH MY!

ARE LLAMAS TICKLISH?

—ADDIE, 4, ARIZONA

I GUESS THERE'S ONLY ONE WAY TO FIND OUT, ADDIE . . .
time to go tickle a llama! We don't actually have
llamas of our own, but Shannon Joy and her mother,
Lori Gregory, do! They run Mountain Peaks Therapy
Llamas & Alpacas, in Washington State. They use their
animals for therapy and education, working with kids
and adults.

Joy says llamas don't laugh, so it had never occurred
to her to think about whether or not they're ticklish.
But as soon as she got our question, her mother ran
out and tickled one of their llamas to see what would
happen.

Turns out, not much!
"It seems as though they
aren't ticklish in the sense
that they laugh," Joy says. "But
I have noticed that when flies
touch their noses or land on
their tails, they tend to swish
the flies away, showing that

perhaps they're ticklish on their faces and their tails." Lots of animals feel ticklish in that way, including humans. When something lightly brushes your arm, for example, you might brush it off because it feels kind of ticklish and uncomfortable. But that's not the same as finding something so ticklish that it makes you laugh.

So, I guess no one's going to start keeping llamas around to laugh at their jokes or have a tickle party. But llamas do make great farm animals. They're often raised for their wool, which can be turned into clothing or blankets. And llamas also make great guard animals! They bravely defend sheep and chickens from wild predators like foxes and coyotes.

HOW DO ANIMALS LAUGH?
—VALLA, 2, ICELAND

OKAY, SO LLAMAS DON'T SEEM TO FIND BEING TICKLED VERY funny, but your question about animal laughter is a good one, Valla. So we asked Alyssa Arre. She works in the Comparative Cognition Laboratory at Yale University. There, scientists look at how humans and our closest animal relatives behave. By looking at how chimpanzees and other apes act, scientists can start to understand what might be uniquely human, and what traits or behaviors we share with other animals.

And guess what? Arre says humans are not the only animals that laugh! "Chimpanzees do something that primatologists, or people who study monkeys, refer to as laughing," she says. "They do it in the same context that humans do. So they'll do it when they're playing or when they're being tickled."

But Arre says a chimpanzee laugh doesn't sound the same as a human laugh. "It does sound a lot different from humans. Very panty. Really cute."

There's another kind of animal that also seems to find tickling funny, and this one might surprise you: rats.

"When you tickle rats, they make this very, very high-pitched sound that you couldn't hear normally," Arre told us. "But if you have a special microphone with the rats, you can hear the high-pitched sound. It sounds like a squeaky swing or something. Again, it doesn't sound like human laughter but the scientists who study this say that it occurs in the same type of behaviors as playing or tickling that human laughter occurs in. So maybe it's something like laughter."

We're sad to say there's no evidence that rats or chimpanzees will laugh at your jokes, though!

WHY DO LLAMAS SPIT?

Shannon Joy tells us it's "very common that people often think that llamas are mean and spitty animals." But she says that's an unfair reputation.

Llamas are part of a group of animals called camelids (which includes camels, alpacas, guanacos, and vicuñas). All camelids can spit, and they do it for a few reasons. Sometimes they do it to show other camelids who's the boss! That's called asserting dominance. Sometimes they do it because they're annoyed with each other.

But they actually don't like the smell or the taste of their own spit—because it's gross! When camelids spit, they're regurgitating partially digested food from their stomachs. The spit is smelly and gooey, so even they don't really like it, and they'll only do it if they feel like they have no choice. They'll often give a warning first, by lifting their chins and pressing their ears back against their heads. Then they might give a little *pffft* sound with a tiny bit of spittle spraying out of their mouths. If you see that, back off!

"Llamas might spit because they are uncertain about you," says Joy. So, just as you should ask an owner of a dog whether it's okay for you to pet it, you should always ask the owner of a llama if it's okay to pet their animal. "Some llamas love to be touched and are very social and very friendly. But some llamas prefer their personal boundary space. And these are the ones that tend to spit on us." So be sure to give llamas their space if they don't seem pleased to see you.

WHY DO SHEEP HAVE CURLY HAIR?

—LEVI, 8, MAINE

KERATIN (SAY: CARE-UH-TIN) IS AN EXTREMELY HARD substance that makes up claws, beaks, feathers, horns, and shells. It's also what hair is made of! Keratin is a protein that forms very strong bonds. If you've ever taken a strand of your own hair and tried to break it in half, it takes a lot of effort—and think about how thin that strand of hair is!

Well, sheep's wool is also made out of keratin (as is the hair or fur of all mammals). But why it's so curly, is a bit of a mystery! There are two theories about what makes hair curly. One theory is that inside a hair, some cells divide more quickly than others, so there are more cells on one side of the hair than the other, causing it to be tighter on one side, resulting in a curl. The other theory is that there are basically two different kinds of cells inside a strand of hair, and those cells are different sizes. One side of the strand has long cells, and one side has short cells. The hair curls in on the side with short cells.

Recent research suggests that the second theory is more likely. Still, there may be more to it than that. By looking at strands of wool from merino sheep, researchers in New Zealand found that hair *does* curl when there are shorter cells on one side of the strand and longer cells on the other side. But it's not always because they're two different kinds of cells. So, more research still needs to be done to be sure!

Now that we know how sheep's wool curls, let's think about *why* sheep have curly hair or wool. Sheep have very thick coats of wool, designed to keep them warm in the winter and cool in the summer. The pockets in the curly wool help to keep outside temperature extremes from getting to the sheep's skin. And sheep's wool is coated in a natural oil, called lanolin, that protects the wool and acts kind of like a raincoat!

DID SOMEONE TURN OFF THE LIGHTS?

Over time, humans have bred sheep to have curlier and thicker fleeces. And they've also bred sheep so they don't shed very much, because people like to collect sheep's wool to turn it into yarn for sweaters, socks, and other kinds of clothes—even underwear!

Most sheep on farms get a haircut once a year. That process is called shearing the sheep. It's basically giving the sheep a shave. If done well it doesn't hurt the sheep, though they don't much like it. Some sheep shearers (a person who cuts sheep wool) can shear a whole sheep in less than two minutes! Ideally, the wool (also called fleece) comes off in one big piece.

It can actually be dangerous for domesticated sheep not to get shorn. Because they don't shed their wool, it just keeps growing. And without human intervention, it could eventually add fifty to a hundred pounds of extra weight to the sheep. All that extra wool could prevent the sheep from being able to get up from the ground, go to the bathroom, or even see!

In fact, one sheep in Australia that was separated from its flock was found with more than eighty-nine pounds of wool! Now that's a *lot* of curly wool!

HOW DOES WOOL BECOME YARN?

—JUDAH, 6, COLORADO

GREAT QUESTION, JUDAH! AND IT'S NOT AS EASY AS YOU might think for wool to go from a sheep's body to your sweater.

Lauren McElroy is a fiber artist who lives in rural Wisconsin and knits beautiful pieces of clothing. You can see her work on her website, Mother of Purl (a purl is a type of stitch used in knitting). Sometimes she makes her own yarn from raw wool. "I lay the fleece out and pick out the parts that are too dirty and matted to use, and I use these pieces in my garden for mulch," McElroy says.

Then it's time to give the rest of the wool a bath, either in the bathtub or outside in a big bucket.

"I use multiple changes of warm water to gently wash the dirt and sheep poop out of the fleece," McElroy says. "After I have changed the water I will use a gentle soap and swish my fleece around in a big tub of water to remove some (but not all) of the lanolin." Remember, lanolin is the oil that sheep produce to help make their wool waterproof. Most yarn processers try to remove all the lanolin, but Lauren likes to leave some of it in. "I want to keep some of the lanolin in the fleece so the wool doesn't get dried out and hard to spin. And it will help the wool last longer when it eventually becomes a sweater!"

The next step is to card the wool with hand carders or wool combs. These look a lot like two hairbrushes with metal teeth. Carding the wool means pulling those curly wool strands with the combs so they all go in the same direction. It's kind of like brushing your hair.

The last step is to take all those pieces of hair and spin them into one long, skinny rope of yarn. Lauren McElroy uses a spinning wheel to twist the individual fibers into yarn. After that, it's ready to be knit into clothing.

"Yarn is so beautiful to me," McElroy says. "I love all the colors, and the feel of the material in my hands. I also like that I can make every single stitch of a piece of fabric completely by hand."

Most wool is not turned into yarn by one person, though. A lot of wool goes from the farm to a mill to be processed, and then spun into yarn by machines. Either way, it takes a lot of work for wool to go from the sheep's back to yours, Judah!

WHY DO GOATS HAVE SQUARE EYES?—ANNIE, 3, MICHIGAN

GOATS DON'T ACTUALLY HAVE SQUARE EYES, BUT IF YOU'VE ever gotten right up to a goat's face, which we're guessing most of you haven't . . . and we're not suggesting you do . . . you'll notice that goats' eyes are a little bit . . .

WOW!

different! It's not the shape of their whole eye that's unique, but rather the shape of their pupil—the black part in the center of the eye. The pupil is what lets light in. Human pupils are round. If you're outside in the bright light of the middle of the day, your pupil will shrink to a small black dot so you're not blinded by all that strong sunlight. But at night, if you're getting up from bed to get a drink of water, your pupils will get as big as they can, to let in all the available light!

Goat pupils act the same way, but they're not shaped the same. Next time you come face-to-face with a goat, check it out—their pupils are rectangular! They're not squares, as Annie wonders in her question, but wide rectangles!

Having a wide rectangular pupil benefits a goat in a couple of ways. For one thing, the shape might help keep the brightest light from the sun out of the goat's eyes while it's grazing. But more importantly, having wide pupils and eyes on the sides of its head gives the goat a much wider field of vision than humans. That means the goat can see if a predator is trying to sneak up on it from the side.

ON THE LOOK OUT

Here's another cool thing goats can do with their eyes: When they lower their heads to chew the grass, their eyes rotate in their heads so they're still vertical, still scanning the horizon! You give it a try. Get on your hands and knees and put your face down like you're trying to munch some delicious grass. With your head all the way down near the ground or the carpet, you can't see much around you, can you? But the goat can still see all around it because its eyes have rotated upward while its head has gone down!

Goats aren't the only animals with horizontal pupils. Horses, deer, toads, and octopi also have this same horizontal pupil shape. Researchers think animals that are usually considered prey animals—meaning they are hunted by other animals—are more likely to have these kinds of eyes. On the other hand, a lot of predators that are low to the ground, such as crocodiles, have vertical slit pupils to help them hunt. So domestic cats, yes; lions, no!

WHY DO GOATS EAT EVERYTHING?
—ANNIE, 7, VERMONT

ACTUALLY, THEY DON'T! GOATS HAVE A REPUTATION FOR being animals that will eat anything and everything. And, if you've ever been to a petting zoo or farm with goats, you know they're likely to nibble your sleeve or a

OOOOH, IS THAT COTTON?!

piece of paper in your hand. But that's just because they're curious animals. Hannah Sessions is the co-owner of Blue Ledge Farm, in Vermont, where she milks about 125 goats to make cheese. "There's a reputation they have for eating tin cans and whatnot, but they're actually incredibly picky," she says. "In our barn, we have to build hay feeders that get the hay up off the ground because they don't like to eat things once they've touched the ground." Picky, picky! Goats that don't have hay feeders will eat off the ground, of course, and they pick and choose different kinds of grasses and plants to eat, including some kinds of plants that are not great for humans—like poison ivy. In some places, goats are used to graze fields, keeping the grass short enough that lawn mowers aren't needed!

CHAPTER 6
WHAT'S IT LIKE TO BE A FARMER?

WHAT'S IT LIKE TO BE A FARMER?

ANIMALS AND PLANTS ARE CRUCIAL TO ANY FARM.
But so are humans! So, what's it like to be a farmer?
We asked one!

We spoke again to our friend Joel McNair at *Graze* magazine to get a better sense of a day in the life of a farmer.

"It's a lot of work!" McNair told us. "Most farmers work long days taking care of their animals and their land. And sometimes they don't make very much money. But most of them like the work, so they still want to be farmers!"

If you're interested in farm animals, you don't have to wait until you're an adult to start learning about taking care of them.

There are several clubs in the United States and Canada that help kids learn farming skills. One of them is called 4-H. (The Hs stand for "head, heart, hands, and health.") 4-H clubs help young kids learn about livestock. They also focus on STEM (science, technology, engineering, and math), healthy living, and civic engagement. While many kids who participate in 4-H are already living on farms and have their own animals, that's not a requirement. If there isn't a club near you, you can start your own, or access their free resources online. Teenagers are eligible to join the National FFA Organization (formerly called the Future Farmers of America). The FFA helps them prepare for careers in agriculture.

If you really want to be a farmer, consider going to college to study agriculture! People do become farmers without going to college first, but a degree program can help you learn more about how to care for animals and run a business. You can also learn about other ways to work in agriculture that don't involve owning your own farm or working on one, like becoming a researcher studying animal science and nutrition, a veterinarian, an animal nutrition specialist, a reproductive expert, a genetics specialist, a farm economist or banker, or an agricultural policy maker. There are a lot of different jobs that are associated with farming.

Reaching out to other farmers can be another important way to learn. McNair says, "If you're interested in seeing if you want to be a farmer, try to find someone who is willing to let you do some work on the farm. Some farms offer formal internships, while others are just looking for some help. Finding these farmers can happen through in-person connections, the internet, and many other avenues. Just keep trying until you find someone who wants to work with you."

CHAPTER 7
HORSES AND THE PECULIAR WAY THEY SLEEP

!

Z z

Z
z Z

z z z

Z Z z

z

WHY DO HORSES STAND UP WHEN THEY SLEEP?—CHARLOTTE, 6, TEXAS

HAVE YOU EVER TRIED SLEEPING WHILE STANDING UP, Charlotte? Not easy—or comfortable! But horses' bodies are designed to allow them to stand up while they sleep so they can get away quickly if they wake up in danger.

Horses don't actually sleep very deeply when they're standing; it's more like napping. When they need to sleep deeply, they do lie down and can sleep for two to three hours. But when they just want to catch a few *zzz*'s, they lock their knees, so they don't have to put much effort into balancing or staying upright, and just doze off. Remember, horses have four legs, which makes balancing a little easier than it would be for humans. There's actually a name for the system that allows a horse to do this: it's called the "stay apparatus," and it's the arrangement of joints, tendons, and ligaments that allows the horse to lock its knees. You might also notice that often a horse has three legs that are totally straight and one that looks kind of bent—that leg is getting a chance to rest while the other three are balancing the weight of the horse (thanks to the stay apparatus). As the horse dozes, it will gradually rotate which leg gets a rest, so that by the time it finishes napping, all four legs have gotten a break!

If you've ever seen a horse try to stand up, it can look a little awkward! It's actually a bit difficult for a horse to get up when it's lying down, so it's beneficial for a horse to already be standing up if it needs to run away.

Horses aren't the only animals that sleep standing up. Zebras (which are closely related to horses), elephants, and even cows can sleep upright. Birds do, too, but usually in a slightly different way. Most birds have special tendons to help lock their talons around a tree branch while they're sleeping, so they don't fall off.

By the way, flamingos act more like horses and elephants when it comes to sleeping standing up, but they do it on one leg! Paul Rose, a flamingo researcher at the Wildfowl & Wetlands Trust, in the United Kingdom, says flamingos actually find it easier to rest on one leg. "If you balance without using your muscles, you actually don't expend any energy whatsoever in keeping still. The weight of the flamingo pushes down through the bones and the joints in the bird's legs, and that means it can stand very energy-efficiently for an incredibly long time." And here's a fun term: When a flamingo is relaxing, it's officially called loafing!

CAN HUMANS SLEEP STANDING UP?

Maybe, sort of. If you've ever fallen asleep in a car, you know that it's certainly possible to fall asleep while sitting upright, especially if you have something to lean against. And videos of children (and sometimes adults) falling asleep in a chair, with their heads nodding forward or back, have gone viral because they're so silly to watch. But there aren't a lot of reports of humans falling asleep while standing up with nothing to lean on. We checked in with a sleep expert, Dr. Lisa Meltzer, to find out more.

"Humans may be able to sleep standing up, but not for very long," she told us. "One thing that happens when we sleep is that we lose muscle tone. So, sleeping sitting up or leaning against a wall helps us to stay balanced. But without that support we would likely fall over." Wow, you wouldn't want to wake up by falling down! Too bad we can't borrow that stay apparatus from the horse!

WHY DO HORSES HAVE HOOVES?

—OLIVIA, 4, INDIANA

AS OLIVIA HAS NOTICED, HOOVED ANIMALS HAVE VERY different feet than humans do. Why is that?

Think of hooves like toenails and shoes combined. Hooves are designed to bear the full weight of the animal, and they're actually made out of the same material as your fingernails: keratin. Remember the keratin that also makes up claws, beaks, feathers, horns, shells, and hair? It is an extremely hard substance, especially when there's layer upon layer of it, as there is in a horse's hooves.

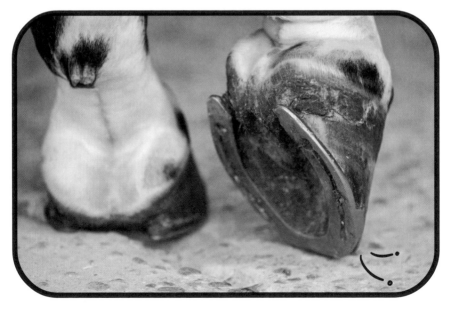

But there's more to a hoof than meets the eye! The hard, outer layer of the hoof, called the hoof wall, is the part that's made out of keratin. Inside the keratin layer is something called a frog! The frog is a spongy material that helps cushion the horse's bones and muscles from the weight and pressure of walking or running, like the shock absorber in a car. The frog also helps with blood flow to and from a horse's foot. Humans don't have frogs, but we do have fatty pads on our heels, the balls of our feet, and our big toes that help cushion our bones when we walk.

The sole is another part of the hoof. But the sole doesn't touch the ground or bear the weight of the horse the same way the frog and the walls of the hoof do.

Just like your toenails, hooves continue to grow throughout a horse's life. In wild animals, hooves get worn down by constant activity, like running around on rough ground. But horses that live on farms need to have their hooves filed down by someone called a farrier.

Horses that do a lot of walking on hard surfaces or who carry heavy loads are also often given shoes—horseshoes! If you've ever seen a horseshoe, it definitely doesn't look like something you wear on your feet. It's a *U*-shaped piece of metal that gets nailed into the bottom of the horse's hoof.

Don't worry—the outer wall of the hoof doesn't have nerve endings. So, if done right, it doesn't hurt the horse when the shoe gets nailed in, though some horses don't like to have their feet handled. The farrier will pry the shoe off every month or two, file down the hoof, and put a new shoe on.

Could you imagine walking on your toenails the way horses walk on their hooves? That would be weird!

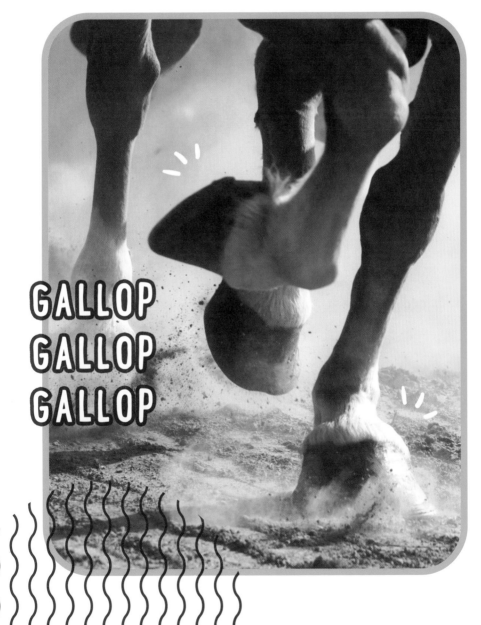

GALLOP
GALLOP
GALLOP

WHAT DO HORSES DO ON A FARM?

There are lots of different kinds of horses, and lots of different things they do on farms! Some people keep horses because they like to ride them, of course, and some riders like to enter competitions with their horses for jumping, hunting, dressage (an event where horses perform precise movements), barrel racing, rodeos, and more.

Some horses are used to help corral other animals. A rancher will ride a horse because it's so fast and tall, and the rancher on the horse helps make sure the other animals, like sheep or cattle, are going where they're supposed to.

LET'S GO!

Big, stocky draft horses are used to pull heavy loads. You might see them in pairs, pulling a sled, logs, or a plow. Before tractors were invented, most farmers had a team of horses or oxen to do that kind of work! Some small farms still do all of their field work, plowing the earth and planting seeds, with horse-drawn equipment. Some farmers use horses because, unlike tractors, they don't need to be filled with gas or other fossil fuels, and because horses can be easier on the land than heavy equipment. People who use draft horses for logging do it because horses can get into areas of a forest that machinery might not be able to reach.

Before cars were invented, riding horses or hitching them to wagons was one of the main ways people got around. When steam engines were invented, they compared the engines to horses to explain to people how powerful their engines were, and the term "horsepower" was invented.

Horses used to provide almost all the horsepower on a farm!

CHAPTER 8
12 ANIMALS (AND INSECTS) YOU MIGHT NOT EXPECT ON A FARM

SO FAR WE'VE COVERED ALL THE ANIMALS YOU EXPECT TO SEE on a farm: chickens, cows, sheep, llamas, horses, and goats. But there are many more animals that are often kept on the farm for a variety of reasons. Some are used as draft power. Some are valued for their fur. Others help with food production.

Here's a short list of some of these species:

BEES: Most crops that produce fruits, seeds, or nuts depend on pollinators (insects, bats, and birds) to fertilize flowers by moving pollen from one flower to another. Nature provides many of these wild pollinators, but their numbers are declining. Now some farmers use the services of commercial beekeepers to pollinate their crops—and then the beekeepers get to harvest the honey! It's a symbiotic (say: sim-BEE-ah-tuhk) relationship, meaning it benefits both bees and humans.

BUZZZZ
BUZ BUZZ

BUFFALO: Water buffalo look kind of like cows, but have big, black curly horns. Ninety-seven percent of the world's water buffalo are in Asia; they are found in smaller numbers in Africa and, a bit unexpectedly, Italy, as a subgroup called the Italian Mediterranean buffalo. The two main groups are river buffalo and swamp buffalo. River buffalo are used for milk production. The milk from these animals is prized for its high fat content. Swamp buffalo produce less milk and are used as draft animals.

In recent years, some American farmers have experimented with raising water buffalo because their milk is used to make buffalo mozzarella, a very expensive cheese! But they aren't in the United States in large numbers.

By the way, when you hear "buffalo," you might be thinking of the great, shaggy bison of the North

American plains because some people call bison "buffalo" in the United States. Around ten thousand wild bison still exist on public lands in the United States. But you can also find bison being raised for meat on ranches, and that's the animal that you might see on a menu as a "Bison Burger."

Some ranches have bred bison and cattle to create an animal called a beefalo. Beefalo are 37.5 percent bison and 62.5 percent cattle.

CAMELS: Camels are kind of like the cows of the desert! In Africa and Asia, nomadic people often keep camels for milk, meat, and to make fiber from their fur. Camels are also pack animals, meaning they can carry heavy loads. People even burn camel poop as a fuel source! Whether camels have one hump (called dromedaries) or two humps (Bactrian camels) depends on where they live. These animals are extremely

valuable to the people who own them because camels can produce milk even in environments where there isn't a lot of water or food, like a desert.

CRICKETS AND OTHER INSECTS: Humans have always eaten insects. But some people predict insects will become a bigger part of the human diet in years to come, as people search for sources of protein that can be produced cheaply, and with less of an environmental impact than animals raised for meat. (It takes a lot less land and fewer resources to graze crickets than cows.)

There are lots of ways to eat insects, from crispy fried grubs to ants in *mole*. Companies are also creating flour made from insects that can be used to make tortillas and crackers, or as protein powder for a bar or smoothie. Maybe give it a try if you get a chance! Just be aware that people who are allergic to shellfish should be careful about eating insects, because most insect bodies and shellfish shells are made of the same material, called chitin (say: KAI-ten).

DONKEYS AND MULES: Donkeys are part of the same animal subfamily as horses and zebras. Donkeys are much smaller than horses and have longer ears and shaggier fur. A mule is the offspring of a donkey father and a horse mother. Donkeys were first domesticated in Egypt and then spread around the world. They are used as pack animals in some countries, especially where keeping horses is too expensive. Donkeys are amazingly strong— they can carry twice their body weight.

HI!

DUCKS AND OTHER BIRDS: When we think of birds that live on farms, we often picture chickens, but ducks are the fourth most popular livestock animal in the world! Most ducks are farmed and eaten in Asia. Other birds farmed on a smaller scale around the world include geese, pheasants, quails, pigeons (also called squab), and guinea fowl. And don't forget the turkey!

QUACK QUACK QUACK

FISH AND SHELLFISH: Most of the fish people eat around the world are wild. This means they are caught in big nets by fishing boats that trawl the oceans. But fish farms are actually on the increase. These fish are raised from eggs and fed by humans—it's a farm, just a watery one! This kind of farming is called aquaculture. Aquaculture is especially big in countries like China, Indonesia, and India, but it's on the rise in the United States as well, where farmers raise shellfish like oysters, shrimp, clams, and mussels as well as salmon, sea bass, trout, and other fish. Sometimes these fish are grown in ponds, sometimes in cages in the ocean, sometimes they are raised in big tanks on land. While the number of fish caught in the wild has stayed the same in recent years, the amount of fish consumed by the world is growing, and aquaculture is making that possible. Some farmers are also experimenting with large-scale aquaponics, where plants and vegetables are grown in the same water used for the fish, creating a system that benefits both types of organisms!

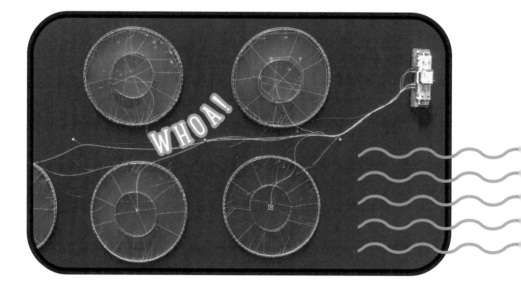

MOOSE: Okay, there's really only two moose farms in the world that we know of. One is in Russia and it's experimental. In the 1940s, scientists in Russia wanted to create a domestic moose breed that could be used for milk, meat, and as a pack animal. They soon learned that while moose are easy to milk, they are not so easy to raise. Now the farm exists mostly as a tourist attraction. The other moose farm is Älgens Hus in Sweden, and it's the only place in the world that sells moose cheese!

OSTRICHES AND EMUS:

Ostriches are the world's largest birds. They don't fly and they're native to Africa, but they can be found on farms all over the world, where they are raised for their meat, hides, and feathers.

Emus are another large, flightless bird, native to Australia. At the end of the twentieth century, a lot of money was invested in emu farming in the United States, with the idea that it was a more environmentally friendly meat source. Emus also produce big green eggs and their fat can be turned into an oil used in skin treatments. But emu meat never really caught on in America, and now there are only a small number of emu farms in the United States and Australia. Rheas are another large bird species that you can sometimes find on farms.

RABBITS: There are over four thousand rabbit
farms in the United States alone. Rabbits are known for their soft fur, and they are raised in farms around

the world for that fur, which can be used to make all kinds of clothes. Most rabbits are killed when their fur is harvested, but angora rabbits are usually plucked, or shaved, the way sheep are sheared. Rabbit meat, farmed or hunted, is also popular around the world.

REINDEER: Reindeer are
an important animal for the Sami people who live near the Arctic Circle. Their

herds of reindeer graze the Arctic tundra, each with a mark on its ear to show who it belongs to! Reindeer meat is eaten in Scandinavia, the United States, and elsewhere. In America, some reindeer are farmed for their meat, while others are used in special events at Christmastime.

YAKS AND OTHER CATTLE SPECIES: Yaks are big hairy cows that live in some of the highest mountain regions of the world, like Tibet. There, nomadic people keep these animals the same way camels are raised in arid (dry) regions. They provide a small amount of milk (much less than for a cow or camel), but they are also used for meat, fiber, and as a pack animal. Yaks are uniquely suited to the thin air in these high elevation areas because they have three times the lung capacity of cows! Other parts of the world also have cattle that are specifically evolved for their region, including gayal, or mithun, a type of mountain cow in Southeast Asia, and Bali cattle, in Indonesia.

CHAPTER 9
THE FARM & YOU!

WE'VE LEARNED SOME COOL THINGS ABOUT FARM ANIMALS in this book, including how chickens lay different colored eggs, why pigs like mud, and how horses are able to sleep standing up.

We've also learned about how farming played a big role in allowing modern humans to create diverse societies where we have all kinds of jobs, hobbies, and activities. The rise of agriculture has led to our ability to create permanent cities and spend our days doing things other than finding, hunting, or growing all our own food. Farming has allowed the world's population to grow and prosper.

Because the world's population has continued to grow, many modern large-scale farming practices have become focused on growing or raising as much food as possible, as cheaply and quickly as possible, in order to feed the over seven billion people who now live on Earth.

In many cases that has meant using the land in a way that is not particularly healthy for the soil, the wild animals, or the waterways on which we rely. The use of fertilizer to help plants grow and pesticides to control damage from insects has introduced chemicals that can pollute our rivers, lakes, and streams and endanger pollinators and other wild animals.

The need to feed so many people has often meant that farms are planting lots and lots of only one kind of crop. This is dangerous, too, because growing the same plants year after year can take nutrients out of the soil. A diverse landscape with lots of different crops is much healthier.

When it comes to animals, there are other challenges. Many farm animals on large-scale farming operations spend their whole lives in small penned-in areas, and are fed special food to help them grow bigger, faster. But keeping so many animals in one place can be bad for the environment and often means the animals don't have very good lives.

SO, WHAT CAN *YOU* DO?

HUMANS DEVELOPED AGRICULTURE TO ADDRESS THE challenges our early ancestors faced in having to spend all their time in search of food. And as we've evolved, we've gotten so good at farming that we were able to create amazing systems to grow more food more quickly. So that means humans are smart enough to balance the needs of our environment alongside the needs of our society. Many people are already working to make a more sustainable food system—a system that can feed the world and protect the environment.

Many farms have been leaders in producing renewable electricity by adding solar panels to their barn roofs and wind turbines to their fields. Some dairy farms solve their waste problems by using cow manure to create electricity! And tractor companies are working on ways to develop electric tractors.

There are also farmers who are trying to diversify

their crops (meaning grow a lot of different crops) and shift to organic agriculture, which doesn't rely on chemical fertilizers or pesticides. Some farms are even trying out techniques to help *reverse* climate change by capturing extra carbon from the atmosphere and storing it in the soil where crops are grown. This is part of what's called regenerative agriculture.

You can help by learning more about the food you eat and where it comes from. That goes for fruits and vegetables as well as the animals you eat. Some people choose not to eat meat (vegetarians), and some people choose not to eat anything that came from an animal, including milk, eggs, and honey (vegans). Some people choose to only eat meat that was humanely raised.

Not everyone has the ability to pick and choose what they eat, but the more you know about your food system, the better the choices you can make.

And if you decide to become a farmer or work in one of the many different jobs that relate to farming, you can help make decisions that protect the world from climate change, ensure that animals get treated fairly, and contribute to a greener and healthier landscape for everyone. Farms are essential to modern human existence, but what they look like in the future will be up to your generation!

CHAPTER 10
"WHEN PIGS FLY," AND OTHER IDIOMS FROM THE FARM

TODAY ONLY 1 PERCENT OF ADULTS IN THE UNITED STATES are farmers. But our farming roots are alive and well in the words and language we use. An idiom is a phrase or expression where the words make little to no sense in a literal way. For instance, you might have heard someone say, "She's barking up the wrong tree." We don't mean the woman is actually barking up the tree. Instead, the phrase has come to mean, "She's looking in the wrong place for an answer." That phrase comes from hunting dogs that would sometimes literally bark at the wrong tree, when the animal they were looking for wasn't there. Many common English idioms relate to farming. Here are a few of them:

"LIKE A PIGSTY"

When your parents say that your room is a pigsty, they probably mean it's a mess. But they're wrong—pigs are actually very neat! (Go back to page 30 for details.)

"SWEATING LIKE A PIG"

We say this when we're really sweaty. But it's not accurate, either! Pigs don't sweat! (See page 31.)

"DON'T COUNT YOUR CHICKENS BEFORE THEY HATCH"

A hen might sit on a clutch (group) of twelve eggs, but that doesn't mean all twelve will hatch! Typically only 75-90 percent of eggs successfully hatch into fluffy chicks, so this idiom warns against relying on something before it happens.

TWEET

"WAITING TILL THE COWS COME HOME"

This expression means that something is probably never going to happen. The origin of this one's a little confusing, too. But some people say cows with lots of tasty grass to eat in their pasture would rather stay out in the field than come home, so if you're waiting for those cows to return to the barn, you'll be waiting a very long time!

I'M NOT MOOOVIN'

"WHEN THE CHICKENS COME HOME TO ROOST"

Chickens can't see in the dark, so once the sun starts to set, they find a high place to spend the night. In a coop, a farmer will set wooden sticks up off the ground for the chickens to sit on. If they're left outside, chickens will find tree branches. This is called roosting, and once a chicken is on its roost, it won't budge.

When we say someone's "chickens have come home to roost," we mean the person is facing the consequences of something they've done in the past.

"WHEN PIGS FLY"

You're right—pigs don't have wings! So when someone says, "When pigs fly," it's a fun way to say, "That'll never happen."

"HARD ROW TO HOE"

Before modern machinery, humans did a lot of field work by hand. Rows of crops were often weeded by people using a hoe. Sometimes one row would be harder than others, leading to the expression "tough row to hoe" or "hard row to hoe." Now most large farms have mechanical or chemical ways to weed their crops, but hoes are still used in gardens—and it can still be hard to hoe a row!

"HAPPY AS A PIG IN MUD"

As we've learned, pigs don't sweat! So on a hot day, pigs love to find a place to wallow, and some nice cool mud is just the place. The mud acts as a natural sunblock and helps keep the pigs cool.

"STUBBORN AS A MULE"

When mules were more commonly used as work animals, they earned a reputation for being stubborn, because they will, at times, resist the commands of their owner. But people who own mules say they've gotten a bad rap. Mules are actually very intelligent and will resist working too hard or doing dangerous things. Sounds like a good quality to us!

NO MORE WORK!

"SEPARATE THE WHEAT FROM THE CHAFF"

This isn't an animal idiom, but it's definitely related to farming. There are a lot of steps between harvesting wheat and making flour. In one of these steps, valuable wheat berries are separated from the chaff, the worthless husk that surrounds them. So this expression means separating the valuable from the worthless.

"PUT OUT TO PASTURE"

When an animal is too old to do its job, it might be put out to pasture to graze and relax. So when we say it's time to "put someone out to pasture," it means it's time for them to retire.

ZZZ

SNOOZE TIME

"HORSING AROUND"

We might tell someone to "quit horsing around" if they're being noisy or silly or rough. This idiom may have come from the way young horses play together, which can be a bit wild.

"PECKING ORDER"

In a flock of hens, one of the hens will establish dominance by pecking at other chickens with her beak. This top chicken wants the best roosting spots and first access to the food. The other hens will sort themselves out into a hierarchy—a system of rank—with some chickens on the bottom and others on top. Now we use this expression to talk about human hierarchies, too!

"BULL IN A CHINA SHOP"

Bulls (male cows) are large and aggressive. They are the last thing you'd want to see walk into a room full of delicate china (dishware). The phrase refers to someone who is clumsy or careless causing a lot of destruction.

GLOSSARY

AGRICULTURE: farming animals or plants for food

CAMELID: a family of animals that includes camels, llamas, and alpacas

CASEIN: a protein in milk that helps give it a white color

DOMESTICATED: describes an animal that can live with humans and is not wild

ENZYME: a substance in the body that can cause a chemical reaction

ETHICS: the guidelines we create to make sure we treat other humans and animals fairly

FARRIER: a person who cares for horse hooves and puts on horseshoes

GRAMINIVORE: an animal that mostly eats grass

HOMOGENIZE: a process that combines milk and cream so it doesn't separate

HUMANE: to treat an animal fairly and with kindness

KERATIN: a hard protein that's in hooves, hair, feathers, horns, and shells

LANOLIN: a natural oil that coats wool and makes it waterproof

MAMMAL: a warm-blooded animal that has hair or fur and can produce milk for its babies

MONOCULTURE: a large area of land planted with only one crop

PASTEURIZATION: heating and cooling milk quickly to kill bacteria

POLLINATOR: an animal or insect that spreads pollen from one flower to another

ROOKERY: a breeding place for birds

RUMINANT: a type of animal that has four stomachs

SOW: a female pig

MORE *BUT WHY!*

AT *BUT WHY*, WE DO A LOT MORE THAN WRITE ABOUT FARM animals. We put out a new episode of our podcast every two weeks—and *you* can be a part of it! We take questions from kids all around the world—just like you—and we find the answers. You can listen to all our episodes at www.butwhykids.org, and that's where you'll also learn how to ask a question of your own that might get used in one of our episodes. We tackle all kinds of topics—whatever *you* are curious about, from how words are invented to why babies take so long to grow up.

BUT WHY IS PRODUCED BY VERMONT PUBLIC RADIO. YOU CAN LEARN MORE ABOUT VPR AT WWW.VPR.ORG.

AND CHECK OUT OUR OTHER BOOK, *DO FISH BREATHE UNDERWATER?*

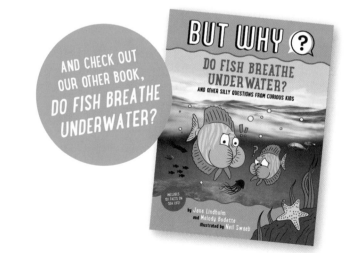